Through the Vally of the Shadow of Death

A Christmas Miracle

Evangelist Patricia Edwards

Through the Vally of the Shadow of Death

THE VALLY OF THE
OF DEATH

A Christmas Miracle

Evangelist Patricia Edwards

All rights reserved. This book is protected by the copyright laws of the United States of America. This book may not be reprinted for commercial gain or profit. The use of occasional page copying for personal or group study is permitted and encouraged. Permission will be granted upon request. Copyright 2023 – Patricia Edwards

Pat's Bio

Evangelist Patricia Edwards is a passionate lover and inspirational teacher of God's word. She has an undeniable and unquenchable calling to ministry that includes disciplining the lost, reaching the broken in spirit, and mentoring young and seasoned ladies in exploring their gifts, talents, and value to the body of Christ. For over forty years, Missionary Edwards has been a faithful member of the Jordan Grove Church of God in Christ located in Dublin, Georgia. She is noted for being an effective change agent in the various capacities she serves. Her varied gifts and abilities have provided her the privilege to serve as an Adult Sunday School Teacher, Vice President of the Jordan Grove Women's Department, Vacation Bible School Director, Dublin District President of the Sunshine Band Ministry, and church organizer of the Thanksgiving Food Drive, along with other local community projects she is engaged in.

Missionary Edwards is a public speaker for civic and religious events and does not hesitate to share the gospel wherever she goes. Because of her servant leadership, God has enlarged her territory to go places and meet people from all walks of life. Evangelist Edwards is a graduate of Savannah State University with a Bachelor's and Master's Degree in Elementary Education. Additionally, she obtained her Educational Specialist Degree from Georgia Southern University in Administration and Supervision. With a long-standing record of a twenty-five-year membership in the Alpha Kappa Alpha Sorority, Inc.,

Evangelist Patricia Edwards' professional career includes being a Teacher, Principal, and Director of Curriculum Instruction for the Dublin City School system. Lastly, she completed the course requirements to be a certified teacher of God's word from the CH Mason Institute in the Northern Georgia II Jurisdiction under Bishop Mark Walden as Jurisdictional Prelate.

Missionary Edwards' ultimate desire is to work in the vineyard and be instrumental in helping someone discover the grace and saving power of the Almighty God.

Dedication

This book is especially dedicated to two significant men who were such an integral part of my life, as well as my dearest mother. To my beloved Father, Ira Edwards Sr., the late Superintendent of the Dublin District COGIC, and my amazing mother, Inez O'Neal Edwards, Emeritus District Missionary of the Dublin District, I revere and honor you as my biological and spiritual parents who instilled Godly principles, as well as moral values in my Christian walk. Thank you for providing and demonstrating a solid foundation of faith and perseverance. Your love helped to shape and mold the very fabric of my existence and the spiritual essence of the woman I am today. I am so proud to dedicate this book to the both of you with much love!

To Alonzo Edwards, my eldest brother of eight siblings, you fulfilled the mission of keeping our family united after the death of our father. Although your untimely death ripped our hearts to pieces, you left a special mark in our lives and those you encountered along life's way. I will never forget the unique bond we shared, the transparency, honesty, humor, and disputes. You always believed in me, respected my beliefs, prayed for me, and loved me unconditionally, flaws and all. I will always remember and cherish you as my eldest brother. Keep watching over Dad as you are both together again!

Acknowledgments

First, I want to thank God for being my source of strength and sustainer of life. It is truly because of Him that I am living, moving, and breathing. God, you are faithful, and your love for me is everlasting. I am so glad that I know you as Redeemer, Savior, and Lord of my life. Your Holy Spirit within guided me through the entirety of this process of penning my first book that personifies the abundance of your grace and mercy. Thank You Lord for all that you have done for me! All the Glory and Honor belongs to You!!!!

Next, I am thankful for my siblings: Sharon, Donald, Steve, Diane, Ira Jr., Anthony, Glen, and the self-acclaimed ninth child, Kesha. Each of you were there in your own special way to pray, support, provide lodging and transportation to appointments, laugh and cry with me throughout the many stages of my journey. Diane, you became a permanent fixture in my life, doing whatever was necessary to keep me encouraged and I will never forget everything you did out of love for me. I am grateful for my nephew Colin, who stepped up to the place in the absence of his Dad, Alonzo, and escorted me to appointments. To all my sisters-in-love: Carol, Tina, Brenda, Teresa, and Debbie; my brother-in love: Elder Andrew Blackwell, you all have been and added blessing!

.

To all of my other nieces, and nephews, as well as other family members, thanks for everything you did to show love for me in such a meaningful way

I have much gratitude for my cousin, Evelyn Carswell, who planted the seed of writing this book. Your faith and belief in me stirred the essence of my soul as I recall the many conversations shared about how God moved on my behalf. Your prophetic voice to write a book so the world could hear my story echoed resoundingly and led me to this place of being a new author. It has been a journey, but God has gracefully been by my side.

Thank you, Evangelist Phreida Liggins, for your mentorship and paving the way for this book to be published. It is simply amazing how God orchestrated our acquaintance! Special Thanks to Amanda Barnhill for undertaking the task of being the publisher of my first book. Your advice in the editing and publishing of my story was so valuable and much appreciated. The role you performed was so critical in the printing of this book.

Thanks to Pastor Bruce Howard, Evangelist Natalie Fields, and many others who spoke a prophetic word concerning the assignment of writing a book and how God will use the book to inspire, encourage, and strengthen the hearts of others in their faith walk.

Finally, to my church family, Jordan Grove COGIC, numerous prayer warriors, friends, coworkers, spiritual moms, and fathers who poured into me and displayed your love of God and entreated me with so much kindness and thoughtfulness, thank you so much. Your labor of love did not go unnoticed.

Table of Contents

Introduction *1*

Chapter 1: The Training Begins *6*

Chapter 2: Abundant Living *18*

Chapter 3: Shifting Seasons *23*

Chapter 4: The Valley Experience *28*

Chapter 5: God's Promise: A Miracle in the Making .. *34*

Chapter 6: Process versus Promise *43*

Chapter 7: Wilderness Experience *47*

Chapter 8: Brokenness *60*

Chapter 9: Enduring Faith *63*

Chapter 10: The Power of God's Word *67*

Chapter 11: Grateful *71*

My Healing Scriptures *76*

A Prayer Of Faith *79*

REFLECTION AND EXPLORATION QUESTIONS .. *81*

Additions To My Life *89*

BOOK REFERENCES *91*

Introduction

"Before I formed thee in the belly, I knew thee; and before thou came forth out of the womb, I sanctified thee and I ordained thee a prophet unto the nations."
Jeremiah 1:5

How profoundly the sound of Jeremiah's words ring in my ears more than ever before. In essence, Jeremiah is saying everything has a beginning, even humanity! It is God that beautifully ordained the origin of life and its existence to be driven by purpose and a unique destiny, no matter the scope, experiences, success, or failures. Just to know that I was a special thought in God's cosmic world even before conception is mind-blowing. The fact that God always begins with his perfect end in mind is a promise that I can hang my hat on.

Throughout life, there are and will continue to be ebbs and flows as we navigate our charted course. But knowing God is the source of all things becomes the challenge mankind must face. My story may be similar or different from yours, but one thing is for certain: we have our own story to tell.

My story commences with the union of my dad and mom; but more specifically during the era of the early 50's, when many African Americans were very much acquainted with the struggles of society, as was my family. I was blessed to be reared by two parents in a strong Christian environment whose faith in God was the foundation on which our home was built. Having meager means and living below the poverty line was an integral component of my childhood. Nonetheless, there were always provisions in the household. We never went without food, clothing, or the basic necessities of life. My father, a very humble and devout rural Pentecostal pastor, stood firm in his faith as he was in his stature. Dad was a little over 6 feet tall, had a muscular physique, and weighed roughly 245 pounds, as I best recall. His presence could be intimidating at first sight, but he was a humble, compassionate, generous, and nonsensical individual. He met and fell in love with a beautiful, young, virtuous woman, Inez, who became his lifetime mate. Dad often stated that her smile was what captured his heart. To the Edwards clan, they were indeed a gift God gave to our family. Under their parentage, boundaries and disciplinary actions, moral values, biblical principles, and nuggets of wisdom were established and were defining moments that helped shape the core of my being. It is my personal testimony that their parenting helped to mold me into the person I am today. Being one of eight siblings, I had many opportunities to learn about healthy family interactions, such as unconditional love, temperance, patience, compromise, meekness, and the purity of godly living. In retrospect, life without this beginning would be so different.

Being the second child in the family, I was the first to go to college in the pecking order of eight, and I landed my childhood dream job as a teacher. That job led me back to Dublin, Georgia, my hometown. Honestly, I would have preferred to be elsewhere, but having a job was a top priority. So Dublin it was! It's interesting that God always has a different plan in mind for those he has set aside to be an instrument for his kingdom. Little did I know that Dublin would be the place where God would fulfill the many plans and promises He had in store for me. God's word in **2 Peter 1:3** affirms this truth: *"According as his divine power has given unto us all things that pertain unto life and godliness, through the knowledge of him that has called us to glory and virtue"*. *(KJV)*

Looking back over my life, I can attest with certainty that God's sovereignty and his providential hand rule throughout life's experiences, be it good or bad. Furthermore, **Romans 6:28** reassures believers that God is at work in everything He allows to happen, no matter the circumstance. Just to digress a bit, allow me to share a spiritual insight on the above scripture. Often, I had heard this familiar scripture read, preached, and quoted. But the spirit focused my attention on the words actually written *(all things work "for the good" to them who love God, to them who are called according to His purpose)*. Like so many others, we tend to skip over phrases that give clarity and the enduring principles the word of God so richly declares. First case in point: I was interpreting the scripture to mean everything will always work for "my good" instead of "the good," which the scripture so plainly states. In the scheme of things, I was narrowing the work of God to always benefit me when it was sometimes intended for a broader audience. I have since learned that things in life do not always feel good, nor are things exclusively designed for my convenience and comfort, but for God's ultimate Glory. Secondly, this promise is only given "to those that love God," those who have the heart of God, who desire to please Him, to those who have an unquenchable thirst of seeking His will, not just to receive his blessings only; but to know God intimately with His purpose overflowing in your life. Thirdly, this passage speaks to the mission that is assigned to those God has called, anointed, and appointed to execute the work of His kingdom. The bottom line is that God will never withhold that which is good if our will is aligned to His plan and will ultimately advance His Kingdom on earth. This golden nugget is central to understanding how God works in good and bad situations.

Through the manifold blessings and recent valley experiences that I will share in this book, the Holy Spirit has enabled me to have a different and deeper perspective on life and living the God kind of way. He has revealed more of the mysteries of his word while stirring up the gifts placed within me. Truly, God has taken me to unfamiliar places and surrounded me with a myriad of experiences that I would never have encountered on my own. His omnipotent hand was always behind the scenes, despite my own personal desires. God was pushing, driving, and compelling me to a higher ground, coercing me out of my comfort zone to cultivate something much greater on the inside. I was unaware that this charted pathway would be the seed to spiritual growth, servanthood, leadership, suffering, refinement, and fruitfulness.

Chapter 1

The Training Begins

Train up a child in the way he should go, and when he is old, he will not depart from it.
Proverbs 22:6

It was August 4, 1951, on a Sunday evening, when a distinguished saved gentleman named Ira Edwards married a beautiful, saintly young lady, Inez O'Neal. To their union were added eight children: Sharon, Patricia, Alonzo, Donald, Stevie, Diane, Ira Jr., and Anthony. We were indeed like the notable TV show in the 70's entitled "The Brady Bunch." There were many issues, conflicts, and times of dispute, but at the end of the day, we were still family connected by blood and bonded by love. We did not have a lot, but we had each other. Growing up as a child, adolescent, and young adult was certainly not a bed of roses for any of us. Yet during those seasons and stages of our life, the blessings and favor of an Almighty God were evident.

My family grew up in the projects on the other side of the railroad tracks. We were, by all established social criteria, "poor." However, blacks who lived in federal housing saw themselves differently during this era. We had all things in common, so there was no economic understanding of poverty, at least in my mind. If there was any lack, someone in the neighborhood would gladly supply the need. A cup of sugar borrowed from one household this week would be a cup of flour given to someone else in need the next week. Comparatively speaking, we were living under the principles of the early churches, as noted in **Acts 4:32**, having all things in common.

Although we were exposed to the term poor, my parents never labeled us as such. Because of their high parental expectations and belief in God's word, stating, *"I can do all things through Christ who strengthens me"* **(Philippians 4:13),** the bar was set very high for the Edwards family. In fact, we were often rebuked for using the phrase "I can't." Subsequently, we were driven to reform our image and self-worth rather than conform to society's cultural beliefs and expectations. We were taught by our parents that any task can be accomplished, lofty goals can be achieved, mediocrity is not acceptable, failure is not an option, and greatness is always within view to acclaim. With that being said, I now know that the moral beliefs, Christian teachings, values, and principles, parental modeling, and personal experiences gleaned were all pieces of the puzzle, working in and of itself to be a launching pad to begin life's journey.

I am still in awe today as I recall snippets of how my father, who had a sixth-grade education, was the sole provider of a family of ten. Dad passionately believed that the training of a child begins in the home and insisted on mom not working so she could attend to the domestic needs of the family. He knew and was confident that he married a wife who was capable of training their children in the fear and admonition of the Lord, and that is exactly what Mom did. I recall many family gatherings where my mother would read bible stories and, in her own way, explain the meaning of what she had read. "Mrs. Inez" (my choice name given to her) knew how to put the fear of God in us, especially when she talked about Hell. Recounting those early years of teaching by Mom and preaching from Dad, I am convinced it had a lot to do with all of the children being saved today and living a successful God-fearing life.

Moreover, my mother had an impeccable ability of parenting, which involved planning, strategizing, influencing, modeling, and balancing the scales of "needs versus wants" to ensure there was always peace, love, and harmony among the flock. She was and continues to be the epitome of a virtuous woman described in ***Proverbs 31:10***. And yes, from a personal perspective, I am amazed how my parents were able to hold everything together for the family with such limited resources. What a tremendous task they both shared in rearing their children. Role models such as my parents and others who understood the significance of a God-centered life were the pillars of our communities back then and are much needed in the healing of our nation today. Regardless of what the younger generation may believe, it does take a village to rear a child!

Here is a good place to paint a more explicit image of my parents and their training, which was our foundation. As mentioned earlier, my dad had a very limited education but was endowed by God with so much wisdom and knowledge on how to be the priest of the home. I often heard it said that there is no manual to parenting. I beg to differ somewhat with that thought because my parents used the Bible as their instructional guide in rearing the family. By no means were they perfect in all their actions, but one thing was sure: their consistency in what they believed never wavered.

I view my dad's call to Godly service very similar to Abraham in the book of ***Genesis 22***, where God called Abraham out from among his kindred and promised blessings that would be attached to his obedience. The Bible is replete with various scriptures that prove God's faithfulness and blessings upon his chosen seed. My dad in his young adulthood was called out from among his family of 13 siblings, who were members of the Baptist faith, to experience God in a new and different way. This call led him to a Pentecostal church, where he received the baptism of the Holy Ghost at the age of nineteen. He and a young man named Sam Bell, someone he fondly spoke of, both received this special gift of the Holy Ghost on a Thursday night at a country church known as Jordan Grove Church of God in Christ. Dad joined this church and was eager to serve in any capacity of need. He was destined for leadership unknowingly. His faithfulness to God and love for God's people positioned him as a servant leader. His initial leadership role was serving as an Assistant Superintendent of Sunday School. Next, among other tasks, he became the Superintendent of Sunday School and several years later was appointed the Pastor of his home church for over fifty-seven years.

However, Dad's first ordination to pastorship was at an even smaller rural church, Rangers Grove Church of God in Christ, located a few miles down the road in Johnson County. As God would have it, this church became the place for Dad to be equipped in the fullness of his call and to learn how to shepherd God's people.

Dad was blessed with a long life, and at the age of 92, he served this congregation for over sixty plus years. I personally witnessed my dad's services rendered to this church in the early 60's. Conversely, he came behind pastors where the sheep were scattered for various reasons and had the tremendous task of rebuilding God's house and restoring hope to the remnant left.

My dad not only pastored the flock but was in the trenches doing any labor necessary for the growth of the church. Daddy and our family were not sustained by what the church could do for us but rather what we could do for the church. It is with this commitment that Dad served two country churches at the age of 92 and kept the unity among both churches until his passing. My Dad, a hero of faith, lived out his belief in serving the Lord until death and the commitment to "wear out" rather than "rust out."

During the early years of Dad's pastorship, the parishioners had very little money but supported him with the harvest from their crops and livestock, which was indeed a great blessing to our family, curtailing grocery expenses. Because of this loving gesture, we were never without food to eat. It was apparent to me as a child that Dad had an amazing zeal for being a servant for the sheep assigned to him. He tenderly nourished them with God's word and lovingly watched over them with the utmost care. I vividly recall Dad also serving his church leaders and submitting himself under their spiritual authority with the same fervor, humility, and the highest level of respect. He was truly a pastor after God's own heart as I witnessed him faithfully serving unselfishly, keeping the assigned sheep close to his heart. Dad was compassionate in his service to the church, spending money he really didn't have to spare and providing resources such as transportation for members who needed a way to church.

You see, my dad was not called to just serve his immediate family only but had a mandate in his life to serve others. Recognizing his God-given gifts, Dad was every bit a visionary. He always saw things beyond what was visible to the natural eye. He saw an old school he attended as a young boy, built for African Americans during segregation, become what is now a Community Center for Jordan Grove Church on the east side of Laurens County. He saw what most would consider an old-school bus and was among the first pastors in our community to provide church transportation for members who did not have the means to get to church. He later saw the need for the purchase of a Trailways bus to be the vehicle for long distance travels to out-of-town revivals, pastoral engagements, and attending jurisdictional conventions. He always had a passion for those who were lacking in resources and made it his personal goal not to deny them any opportunities related to the church.

Dad was progressive in his thoughts as he envisioned blacks being owners of properties and businesses. He demonstrated this belief with the purchase of properties for the churches he pastored. Over the years, his vision led to the expansion and renovation of these churches into the beautiful structures they are today. Additionally, Dad saw the need to mentor young men, whether they were in or out of the church. He poured into the lives of many as he fathered with his wisdom, compassion, and generosity. Dad often used his sense of humor to give pointed instructions. His two endearing quotes: **"*I can see more over the wall than you can see on the wall" and "I can help you if you let me.*"** Without question, those who knew my dad would agree on both accounts he was so-ooo right!

Mrs. Inez, my mom, has her own impressive resume of serving her family, the church, and anyone she came in contact with. Mom, unlike Dad, was a social butterfly. She never met a stranger and always had an uncanny way of speaking hard nuggets of truth that could leave a bitter taste if not received in love. Mom enjoyed her role as a mother to our family, even during difficult times. Now, this special lady is a "tough cookie" mixed with grace and kindness, which has given her resiliency over the years. Even now, as she spends her elderly days in the nursing home at the age of 95 during the writing of this book, she is yet graced with the endurance to overcome her day-to-day-issues. When I look upon her now, I see immeasurable strength that only God can provide.

My mother's roots are from a Pentecostal background. As a matter of fact, the church we grew up in started out of her parents' home. Pop and Big Ma, affectionately called by the grandchildren, were rooted and grounded in righteousness and holy living. They were among the pillars of Zion Hope Church of God in Christ in the Dublin area, which became the beginning of the Edwards children's church roots. My grandparents' love for God and his people was embraced and demonstrated by my mother as we observed how they faithfully served in the church. Mom, in particular, emulated many of the servant-like qualities of her parents and taught us through examples of how to do so as well.

Aside from religious training and activities, Mom also prepared us to go out and present ourselves in the larger community as valuable citizens. She was intentional in her efforts to ensure that we were well-groomed and dressed appropriately for school or church. She dressed us as if we were models in a Sears Roebuck catalog, even though we wore second-hand clothing. She and Dad were also arrayed in clothing that made them look like a million dollars, which was certainly not the case as she shopped in thrift stores for bargains during that period.

Mom was confident and never faltered to take on any task she was given. I remember very fondly when she was elected to be my class PTO President in elementary school. Admittedly, I was fearful about her ability to handle the responsibility she was to assume, but not "Mrs. Inez"! She was certain of her capabilities to do any task with God's help, and she did! But more importantly, she was demonstrating to her children that we, too, could be leaders and make a mark in society on a civic level, which many of us were able to do.

Mom's highest educational attainment was a year of college. Her intention was to become an Interior Decorator, but marriage set her on a different path. Entering the workforce late, Mom started as a maid at a 4-H Club facility, next as a cook in the school system, and later worked for the Laurens County Health Department, beginning as a maid. However, her inner drive, intellectual capabilities, and interpersonal skills destined her for a better position within this agency as she became the first African American to hold the position of a Family Planning Coordinator for young teenage girls. This job provided mom with a higher salary, good benefits, and a great retirement plan. Having accomplished her goal of not settling for less, she provided a living example of the tenacity it takes and the work ethic required to create your own job opportunities, as well as a legacy for others to follow.

With this same passion, Mom pushed our family to be more than we saw within us. Mrs. Inez was indeed the family's finest jewel. She was our greatest cheerleader as children; she was dad's confidant and First Lady of the two churches he pastored and a role model for other families in our neighborhood. With a humble spirit, Mom proudly shouldered her responsibilities with grace and honor. She was delighted to work alongside my dad in ministry and be the leading lady of the saintly women she represented. Many of the church women often mentioned how mom's sidebar conversations: tidbits about rearing children, reprimands about godly character, teachings on being chased keepers of the home, and other personal and spiritual matters she felt the need to address" were instrumental in their Christian maturity.

Conversely, you can't even imagine the countless times she pulled each of her eight children to the side on many occasions for one-on-one conferences to encourage, rebuke, instruct, correct, and share wisdom for successful living. This certainly happened when we were children but did not cease after we were grown adults.

Sharing the intricacies of my parents' lives shows how every facet of who they were helped to structure my family's spiritual existence. Their character, legacy of faith, service, loyalty, and determination are the building blocks on which I personally stand today. Had I not seen my parents' unyielding faith during their growing and developing days as believers despite good and bad times, I shudder to think what my fate would have been in going through the many trials and temptations ahead for me.

It would be robbery if I didn't credit the church community, especially my dad's congregants, who were vital components of support and training in my early stages of discipleship. The devout deacons and wise-spirited mothers who were seated in what was called in our black churches the "Amen Corner" were suited and armed with prayers, fasting, and equipped for spiritual warfare. Their decree was that Satan would not steal, kill, or destroy the church under their watch. This holy band of saints literally lived ***Ephesians 6:10,*** which states to put on the whole armor of God.

Moreover, the church leadership and laity taught the younger saints like myself to "fight the good fight of faith." These saintly patriarchs and matriarchs were very well acquainted with struggles that came from every side. Their lives were living, breathing testimonies of how God opened doors, made ways, healed bodies, kept them from harm, as well as gave them supernatural strength to endure the hard times. Aside from the myriad of biblical personalities in the

Old and New Testaments, the present-aged saints' nurturing, teaching, and training provided real-life, tangible experiences of trusting God even during the most difficult times in life. Their testimonies attested to the greatness of our God and affirmed that there is nothing too hard for Him. They taught us through their examples of how to stand on the promises of God's word. Subsequently, I can see how all of the preparation and training were carefully crafted by God for my personal faith walk and for his ultimate Glory.

Chapter 2

Abundant Living

Beloved, I wish that, above all things that ye prosper and be in health even as your soul prosper.
3 John 1:2

Abundance is every believer's portion; subsequently, we do not have to settle for anything less. It is the will of the Father to give good gifts to His children. Living an abundant life is one of the many precious promises God has given to those who choose the way of righteous living. Strong's concordance defines the word abundance in Ephesians 3:20 as exceedingly, very highly, beyond measure, more than enough, a quality so abundant as to be considerably more than what one would expect or anticipate. In short, abundance means an overflowing stream of resources in your possession. For example, Jesus promises a life far better than we could ever imagine. This biblical understanding was a blind spot in my life since I was using the world's definition of abundance to define who I am and what I had.

The real truth is that abundance is less about possessions and more about the relationship with the one who is the creator of all things. Through my spiritual development, I discovered a significant doctrinal truth: an intimate relationship with Jesus starts your journey to abundance.

And just to be clear, abundant living is much more than accepting Christ as your personal savior and receiving "ALL OF THE BLESSINGS WITH YOUR NAME ON IT." God's abundance is so much more than that and entails all dimensions of human life. God's abundance embodies the grace, sufficiency, and endurance to deal with unfavorable circumstances and yet remain steadfast even when everything seems to be falling apart. The Bible so clearly states in ***Matthew 7:13-14*** "narrow is the gate and difficult is the way that leads to life"; thus, many don't travel this path. In other words, another dimension of abundant living is the sufficiency we find in God. It can be viewed as the road that few travel because it is often full of challenges, uncertainties, questions, persecutions, loneliness, and suffering. Yet, in spite of the above, it yields immeasurable fruit in pursuit of the promises of God. Jesus clearly stated in ***John 10:10*** that the thief comes to steal, kill, and destroy, but He has come that we may have life more abundantly. In Jesus, we have all that we need, and our faith pushes us to that higher ground when we find ourselves in difficult spaces.

Over the years, and even as I pen this book, I am defining and redefining what abundant living is all about through the eyes of God. Admittedly, when I gave my life to Jesus and really got serious, I was a novice at this notion of being saved. The era I grew up in was a Pentecostal, bible teaching, handclapping, foot-stomping, tongue-talking church that kept the children and new converts at the altar, tarrying before God for salvation. Children like me were often commanded to come to the altar to be saved. In other words, we did not have a choice of whether we wanted to come to the altar or not. Therefore, most of us did not take our salvation seriously.

On the other hand, adult converts, or those who desired to be saved were extended an open invitation to come to the altar. This action was something I didn't quite understand as a child of not having a choice. But one thing is for sure: the persistence of the older saints kept my heart tender towards God. And yet, at times, I was void of commitment. In short, I was confessing salvation until my fleshly desires drove me in another direction. Honestly, I wanted to be a part of both worlds, but I knew that was not God's way and certainly not the road to abundant living.

It was 1972, my second year of college when I stopped running and accepted Christ as my Savior "for real" this time. No, this decision was not without an internal struggle. I was away from home, free to do anything I desired, no longer under the watchful eyes of my parents and people who knew my family background. However, the seed of God's word had been planted, and there was always some level of restlessness within. To soothe my soul, I would attend the campus church or other nearby churches on Sundays. For me, attending church never posed a problem because I was accustomed to this routine growing up as a child. Yet, no matter what I did or did not do, an inward struggle made me uncomfortable and discontent with my life. Whenever I went to certain places, I stood out as different even though I was trying hard to fit in with my surroundings. I recall times when I would literally be singled out with words such as "You don't belong here." "What? Are you kidding me?" Was there some stamp on my head that gave this revelation, or was it my own discomfort and conviction that was on display? Whatever it was, sometime later, I gave up the fight. One Sunday night during my summer break from college, I surrendered to God's invitation of salvation at my dad's church. I recognized my own need to run to God, which was the best decision I ever made. I share this testimony only because life became so much better for me. Unquestionably, I was finally in the place where I belonged.

Living a saved life as a young adult was so exciting during this time. I was full of energy and ready to tackle the world. Being involved in many of the church activities kept me focused. Studying God's word became a passion of mine. I was eager to learn and grow in the faith. My commitment, enthusiasm, and willingness to serve provided an opportunity for me to become an assistant Sunday School teacher under the watchful eyes of Mother Louonie B. Eagle, who was the Sunday School teacher of the adult class. Years later, this precious, admirable, well-respected, saintly mother passed the baton to me unexpectedly. The training I gleaned from this mother will always be an integral part of my spiritual development. Being a servant of God, then and now, is still a delight. In the broader scheme of things, God was truly blessing me in every way: in the church, on my job, and in the larger community.

Life was good, even with the little hiccups I would experience at times. I was single, saved, favored by God, financially secure, and self-reliant. I felt as if I could conquer the world. There was nothing or no one that could get in my way. As I now reflect on these early beginnings, I can see how God was providing, shielding, and building my faith as I tasted the goodness of His GREATNESS. Even though there were bitter and sweet moments, my good days far outweighed the bad days. God's grace was always upon me to bring me out during the brief moments of personal despair. In retrospect, these were my infant years in Christ and the crawling stages of my spiritual growth as I was secure in the hands of Jehovah God. At this juncture, I had no idea that I would encounter a deeper knowledge of God or that I would face another layer of abundance, which would include some life-altering events where my faith would be tried even more, the nights would be longer, and my very own life would be hanging in the balance.

Chapter 3

Shifting Seasons

"Behold his soul which is lifted up is not upright, but the just shall live by faith."
Habakkuk 2:4

God often uses his written word to personally speak to me and reveals insightful thoughts of His plans and my future. This scripture in Habakkuk was what I was inspired to read on the first day of January 2020. The last phrase of verse four, "the just shall live by faith," was a prophetic message for the coming year, although I did not know to what extent. Many others in the body of Christ had their personal declarations for the year, such as "2020: Perfect Vision" or "The Year to Receive Double for Your Troubles." While these phrases were full of much hope for the coming year, I could not renounce the word that God had placed in my spirit. I can certainly see how God was preparing me for the trials ahead that would require my faith to be exercised at a deeper level than ever before.

The year 2020 was full of challenges and unforeseen occurrences. A look in the rearview depicts our nation facing a pandemic, COVID-19, which became a rapid, global spread of this unprecedented disease and the loss of countless lives

More specifically, the church was impacted by this deadly virus, causing the demise of the highest tier of leadership in churches, as well as many of our beloved saints and family members. Suddenly, our church doors were closed, and believers were forced to trust God for creative ways of ministry. Simultaneously, everything in the secular world of operation was shut down as if God himself was warning all of us to "stop, listen, and repent." What we once knew as a normal life had been drastically interrupted and left us unprepared for what was ahead.

God was calling us to question as He did Adam in the garden when he had fallen from grace. The questions I believe God is asking us even today are very similar: "***Where are we?***" "***How did we get off course?***" ***What is our work really about?***" You see, I believe God desires more from us, especially the body of believers. And as was depicted in the book of Habakkuk, our lack of obedience to God would surely land our feet on grounds where our faith would be tested. Our only way out and source of survival would come through God. Thus, in the days ahead, prophetically, the just would have to live by faith to overcome the attacks of the enemy.

Unknowingly, in 2020, I had my own personal battles and would have to embrace the principle of "THE JUST SHALL LIVE BY FAITH!" First of all, I lost my brother-in-law in April and my beloved father in December of 2020. Both were unexpected deaths due to health issues not related to

COVID-19. Their deaths were the closest I had been to experiencing the loss of immediate family members in some time. The pain, grief, and sorrow were undoubtedly heavy weights to bear. Secondly, in September of that year, I had a second knee replacement, revealing my own hidden health issues. And thirdly, the various challenges I would encounter on the journey to victory and healing put me in a very unfamiliar and discomforting space that gave impetus for the writing of this book.

In other chapters, I will share details of the trials I endured as I battled to keep my faith alive while trusting God through the process. Honestly, there were many moments during my valley experiences when I felt like my world was spinning out of control. But I had to keep fighting! I knew my faith was being tested as never before. Dealing with the pandemic, being sheltered from what was considered normal settings, coping with the loss of immediate family members, and maintaining a functional and healthy lifestyle would no doubt be the challenges ahead for me. Indeed, my season was shifting!

Preparation

June 3rd, 2020, was my 67th birthday. For some reason, it felt different. Not really sure why, but it did. On this special day, I was thankful that God had graced me with another year of life. But I also was reminded on that day how I lost my dearest and closest friend, Patricia Stuckey, at the age of sixty-two. Since her death, I have become more sensitive to how precious life is and how quickly it can be taken away. Unfortunately, in 2012, my best friend, Pat Stuckey, was stricken with a blood clot to the brain on December 1st, my dad's birthday, and died on December 3rd, my sister's birthday. As God would have it, my friend's death in the month of December, eight years later, would be the timeline that I encountered my own serious health battle. The timing of her impending death parallels my timeline of a miraculous healing.

Until the age of sixty-six, I considered myself very healthy. By medical terms, I was a little overweight had a slightly elevated blood pressure and a borderline cholesterol level that required medication and monitoring, respectively. I also had arthritis in some of my joints, eventually leading to two knee replacements. Although I am not minimizing these health issues; I just considered them common ailments that people my age, more often than not, battle against. But more importantly, there was nothing in my medical history that I thought raised a serious red flag of concern.

Please understand me; I knew that I was by no means a health buff, even though I did exercise routinely, tried to have better eating habits, lost a few pounds, and kept my scheduled medical appointments. I earnestly was not aware of a serious health condition.

Hypothetically, if I had been asked to rate my overall health on a scale of 1 to 10, with 10 being the optimum health, I would have given myself a rating of 8, or so I thought. To my surprise, it was during this same year, 2020 that I had a face-to-face encounter of how quickly a person's health could change without warning or how certain symptoms can be ignored or not even present that can drastically change one's status of good health. That, my friends, is what happened to me.

Chapter 4

The Valley Experience
"The Lord is my shepherd. I shall not want."
Psalms 23

God's love for me as one of his sheep that was slowly drifting towards the valley of death became the core of my existence to live. I remember very distinctively how deaf toning the sound was when I received the report from my MRI procedure on a Friday evening, December 5th of 2020 that a mass was discovered on my brain. The on-call physician stated that the MRI results also indicated swelling on the brain for which medication had been prescribed and an appointment scheduled in Macon, a fifty-mile journey from my hometown, to visit a neurologist at 9:00 a.m. on the following Monday. The doctor who gave me this report was filling in for my primary physician, Dr. David Tate, who left instructions to contact me when the results of the MRI had been determined since he would be out of town that weekend. The on-call doctor and his nurse displayed the best bedside demeanor with their kind, gentle, and genuine concern for my health. The last word from this call was the doctor's nurse, who said, "I will be praying for you." Those very words pricked my heart as she spoke, displaying her faith to pray about my situation, someone I didn't know and have never seen even until this day. However, the calm and yet urgent sound in her voice convinced me this was a serious matter. After getting off the phone, everything felt numb. I was undoubtedly shocked by the news, in disbelief that something like this could happen to me. After all, I was one of God's chosen vessels. He would never allow something this unfortunate and life-threatening to occur. I immediately phoned my sister about this news and recounted all that the doctor had shared, specifying that I did not need to be left alone awaiting my Monday appointment with the neurologist scheduled in Macon.

After hearing the news, family members were suddenly on the scene to hear the specifics of my issue, comforting me with their prayers, encouragement, and assurance that I was going to be alright. Ironically, I was often the one who would encourage, comfort, and reassure others during their difficult times. Now, the role was reversed, and I needed someone to build my faith with fervent prayers and support. Following the doctor's instruction, my sister, Diane, spent the night with me, attending to my needs and purposely diverting attention from the thoughts that weighed heavily on my mind with light conversations and nuggets of faith words to soothe my despairing soul.

Later that night, when I finally drifted off to sleep, I was awakened by preaching on the phone in the adjacent bedroom where my sister was sleeping. My sister had a recorded message spoken by a prophetess, unknown to me, whose text came from the book of **Psalms 40:2,** where David found himself in a dilemma that was dreadful as well. The Psalm states, *"He brought me up out of a horrible pit, up out of the miry clay and set my feet on a rock and established my going."* This verse was what I so desperately needed to hear in my moment of emotional despair. As a result of hearing the authoritative and powerful word of God, I was moved to action. **Romans 10:17** affirms that faith comes by hearing and hearing by the word of God. With renewed faith, I got up from my bed and went into the bedroom where my sister was sleeping.

With tear-stained eyes, I said to her, let's pray. This word had given me renewed hope and the faith to fight as I stood on his spoken promises. That night, I remember holding my sister's hand in agreement that God was going to bring me out of my horrible pit. As we closed the prayer, I acknowledged my fears and said, "Lord, help me not to disappoint you through this process of walking by faith." I knew that God was with me, and I had to totally rely on Him to get me through this pit experience.

Thinking back to my second knee replacement, I began to see symptoms that were totally different from my first knee replacement. The surgery was already scheduled for September 3, 2020, only a few days after my father's death and burial. By this time, I was using a walker to help me with my balance and to prevent any possible falls. My Dad knew before his death that this was a planned surgery and was encouraging me not to keep putting it off because he saw how it was affecting my mobility, even though I made few complaints. But more significantly than that, Dad, being a man of God, knew that there were deeper health issues I was not aware of. It was only after his death that I was told by my brother, Alonzo, who has since died from a massive heart attack one year after my dad's death, that he had been given instructions to make sure he took good care of me.

Although my brother is no longer living, he did follow my dad's command. He was broken in spirit over my dad's death and had no foreknowledge of the seriousness of my health, but he made every effort to see about me.

Before the Diagnosis

During my period of rehab for the last knee surgery was the first evidence of health issues beginning to surface. After four weeks of therapy, I was not pleased with the way I was walking, even with devices. My family noticed physical changes in how I was using my left arm, which resembled a stroke-like victim. Additionally, the rehab therapists were questioning things of concern and my lack of coordination. Eventually, I was told that my walking issues were unrelated to the knee replacement but could possibly come from my back or, worse yet, a possible stroke. Ross, one of the therapists assisting me, did a quick assessment to determine if I had been experiencing previous headaches, blurred vision, or strength loss.

None of these indicators were noticeable symptoms, although other signs were evident, such weakness on the left side, some cognitive delays while driving and performing routine tasks, along with balancing issues, all of which I attributed to be possible side effects from my knee replacement or medications. Nonetheless, a referral to see my primary physician was recommended and was the initial beginning of my diagnosis.

My primary doctor's assessment was similar to the physical therapist which was a possible mild stroke during my second knee replacement. I questioned how this could have happened or without post-surgical advice.

These answers still remain unclear, but the most important factor was that my doctor wanted to get to the root of the problem by ordering an MRI to be done the following day, which was Friday, December 5th. I had never experienced the nosiness of having an MRI done. The bang, bang, chirp, chirp, cling, clang, beep, beep, and other unfamiliar sounds overwhelmed me at the least. I could feel my nerves getting anxious with each succeeding sound, so my solution was to recite scriptures that I had memorized over the years. Scriptures such as ***Psalms 121:1,*** *"I will lift my eyes unto the hills from which cometh my help";* ***Psalms 27,*** *"The Lord is my light and my salvation whom shall I fear";* ***Psalms 34,*** *"many of the affliction of the righteous, but the Lord will deliver him out of them all."* I cited scripture after scripture, as many as came to mind, over and over, until I was physically released from this dreadful cylinder that enclosed my body, as well as the irritating noise seemingly fixed in my mind. When done, I left, thanking God that this experience was over. I had an unspeakable sense of peace and calmness that evening until around 5:00 p.m. when I received the results of the MRI revealing a mass on my brain.

Earlier thoughts that were secretly hidden long before things began to surface concerning my health were the giant I was facing. Not really understanding the space I was in, I vividly remember several months before the diagnosis and all of the other occurrences that followed, sitting on the edge of my bed one morning as I looked into the mirror for a glimpse of my appearance, seeing a different reflection. The person was indeed me but unrecognizable: tearful eyes filled with floods of emotions, frail in body, weary in soul, and confused in mind, searching for answers I did not possess. I knew I had to be rescued. It was me, "O Lord, standing in the need of prayer." I was in the valley of despair. Fighting with all that I had and all that I knew was simply not enough. Trying to be strong at my deepest point of weakness.

I was concealing symptoms beyond what my family had witnessed and being defensive about any inquiries of concern. I had gotten to the place where God wanted me. A place of total surrender at His feet of mercy. It was only then that I heard these comforting words. "I will be with you".

Chapter 5

God's Promise: A Miracle in the Making

Thou anointed my head with oil, my cup runs over.
Psalms 23:5

The first week of December 2020 will always be etched in my memory as eventful and full of what I call "God Moves." This week was God's timing to unveil my hidden health issues and allow me to witness His supernatural power that would lead me to my miracle. The timing of events was notable, providential, unsettling, amazing, and very explicit, to the point of journaling to keep a written record of the mystical and unusual occurrences. God had set things in order for my miracle to take place and for me to finally see his providential hand through all the experiences I encountered. It was as if God suddenly stepped on the scene and became my very present help, although my faith knew He was always there.

As I rewind the script back to November 29, 2020, a Sunday night, just before retiring for bed, I remember anointing my head with oil, a practice of my Pentecostal roots. About a fingertip of oil was left in a tiny bottle placed on my top dresser. To this day, I am not really sure where this source of oil came from or even how long it had been placed there, but, in spirit, I was drawn to release my faith in trusting

God for my personal healing. I recall pouring the oil in the center of my head, not knowing that God was revealing the root of my problem through this action. During the night, I was prayerful and was open to hearing God's voice or some sign from the spirit for my next step. Amazingly, God did just that. I was instructed to start each day with praise and worship, to pray, and to sanctify my house from adversarial unseen spirits and forces of darkness that were designed to take me out.

Convinced that this was my assignment, I got up the next morning following God's command. Pandora music became the worship leader as I joined the praise of songs that I heard. The songs were God-ordained because each daily song ministered to my present needs as I attentively listened to the lyrics. I could hear God say that the worship melodies would aid in sanctifying and cleansing the atmosphere of my home. The next thing would be prayer time of communing, repenting, confessing, and decreeing my expectations before God. I had to open my mouth and say aloud the declarations of His word. This order for my day still continues as I obediently follow his instructions.

On December 1st, my dad's birthday, I got up with praise and worship. Feeling melancholy with different emotions running through my mind because I was unable to wish my dad a happy birthday and do our family celebration. I knew I could not remain in that frame of mind, so I purposely refocused and made the best of that day. The next day, I called my sister to invite her on a shopping trip to Macon, which we really enjoyed. On December 3rd, Diane's (my sister) birthday, I went to an Italian restaurant to celebrate her special day with family members.

However, it was that evening that I experienced two strange symptoms in my family's presence: stumbling just before I got to our assigned table and later losing my balance while sitting in a chair as I was reaching to pick up my napkin from under the table. Of course, my family was startled as I was trying to keep from falling out of the chair and from making a big scene. Instantly, God had a strong, muscular-built African American young man assigned as our waiter who saw my dilemma and rescued me just in the nick of time. I was literally unable to sit myself up in the chair and was floor-bound. But this young man had a bear hold on me that prevented a devastating fall. You can't tell me that my God isn't an "on-time God." This was another "God Move" showing His protective power over me. After leaving the restaurant, my sister-in-love, Carol, insisted on walking with me back to where my car was parked. As she unlocked the car door, I got in on the passenger side with no thought of this mindless act until she questioned me about what I had just done. I simply laughed aloud because I was supposed to be driving home. Another example of unclear thoughts that I secretly kept. Nonetheless, God had his hands on me with the care he provided on a consistent basis.

Before the above incidents, I had actually gone to work earlier that day, performing my daily tasks with no difficulties.

But honestly, getting dressed for work or going anywhere had become a burdensome chore, which was something I did not disclose to my family. For some time, I was feeling weakness on my left side, my left foot was slightly twisted, making it hard for me to keep on shoes. I often would put my undergarments on backward, including my dresses and blouses, not realizing this until my clothing felt awkward. Basically, I had accepted a new norm for my life without realizing that these were symptoms of a greater problem.

Since then, God revealed to me one night after the surgery that the pressure of the mass against my brain was causing me to do things in reverse order and had affected my cognitive skills. Even my driving ability to use the turn signals, parking within boundaries, processing when it was time to stop or go at traffic lights, and going past streets that I was very familiar with to get to my destination were symptomatic problems I was experiencing. It's apparent now that many of my activities then were mindless actions.

December 4th was my scheduled appointment with my primary physician to discuss symptoms shared by my therapist about his observation. My physician was concerned about the left side weakness and ordered an MRI that I took on that Friday, December 5th. Later that night, I started to feel strange sensations running up and down my left side. I remembered that the on-call doctor had advised me to go to the emergency room immediately if anything felt differently in my body after taking the prescribed medication ordered for swelling. So early Saturday morning, around 2:00 a.m., I had my sister take me to the hospital. Praying on my way, I was asking God to have mercy on me and, if anything was seriously wrong, to just allow me to be transported to Macon rather than wait as I had been earlier advised by the physician.

As it turned out, God's plan was different. I went through a series of tests that morning, which revealed there may be bleeding on my brain. Because of the seriousness of the matter, the ER physician, Dr. Johnson, felt I should be transported to Macon immediately, which was the nearest hospital and later left my bedside to make arrangements for my transportation. Unfortunately, when he returned, I was told that he was unable to get me into Macon, Augusta, or Savannah hospitals because of the COVID-19 restrictions. Here I was again faced with another dilemma! These hospitals had no more room for incoming patients. Lying on the bed early that morning, my question was: God, what am I to do? I felt abandoned because things in my mind were not lining up to get the serious care I needed. But God Almighty was working on my behalf!

Unknowingly to me, Dr. Johnson was taking my case seriously and had made contact with Emory for entrance into their hospital, although they too were under COVID restrictions and also had a no admittance of new patient policy in place. Nonetheless, God had opened a closed door as he somehow got me admitted into Emory, the best hospital of choice. God had not abandoned his child, which was another "God Move." In fact, He had set things in place to have the right doctor, making the right connections to get me the best medical service required. Truly, God had dispatched his angels from heaven to ensure I got the necessary care despite the odds working against me. With praise in my mouth and peace in my spirit, God had come to my rescue again, as I remembered He had promised me that He was with me.

After arriving at Emory that Saturday evening, I had to wait in the ER lobby area until a room was available. I was later rolled to intensive care, where I was blessed to have a private attending nurse named Sara from Trinidad who cared for me like a mother attending to her child. I vividly recall her coming into my room periodically to check on me as she performed her routine tasks. Her soft-spoken voice, in her ethnic dialect, was calming and very comforting as she reassured me with conviction that I would be okay. She would occasionally engage in brief conversations, displaying a professional yet interpersonal demeanor.

On Sunday, December 6th, I was rolled down to be assessed by a neurological team who would determine specifically the nature of my problem and the required surgical procedure.

Admittedly, I was having an emotional meltdown while waiting for the surgical team to begin their evaluation process. Lying in the waiting area felt like hours, which was not the case. It was really a short period of time as I was fighting back unwanted tears and fears. Sara, my attending nurse, was with me during this waiting period. I am truly convinced that Sara was one of God's human angels. She was a Christian who believed in the power of prayer, and while waiting, ministered to me, reminding me that God is the chief physician and that I was in the best hands with Emory's surgical team. This precious lady never left my side, clenching my hand with assurance and compassionate words that God was with me as she gently wiped the steady flow of tears from my eyes.

Apparently, I had been lightly sedated because I didn't remember anything until I recovered and saw the surgeon, Dr. Jeffery Olsten, standing over me to tell me the results of their assessment. His findings were that the mass was a tumor centralized in my skull area and was pressing on my brain, causing undue pressure. His medical advice was to remove the tumor centralized in my skull rather than allow it to remain for safety reasons. Of course, I had to give medical consent for surgery, which was scheduled the next day on Monday. He also had a general idea of the type of tumor but would not be certain until after the tumor was removed and sent off to the pathologist to determine the type and grade. As it stands, I had to go through stages of healing. The first task was to remove the tumor.

There were so many "God Moves" throughout this journey, which is another reason for writing this book. Another God moment was the angelic care I was given by everyone that was assigned to me. As I was lying on the gurney, having heard that surgery would take place on Monday, a female staff member who apparently was on the surgical team voiced out loud that "her sister will be allowed to be here on Monday for the surgery." She emphatically stated, "Every sister needs their sister in moments like this." Interestingly, I was never introduced to this staff member, but apparently, she had the authority to make exemptions to the COVID restrictions related to visitors. She called my sister after their assessments the same day, around three o'clock that Sunday, to find out how soon she could arrive in Atlanta that afternoon before my scheduled surgery the next day. And yes, God made it possible for my sister, Diane, to be with me. When she arrived, the people who were unaware of the exceptions that had been made were following their routine procedure of denying entrance into the hospital. When my sister explained she had been notified by the doctor to come and be with me and identified the staff member's name that gave her permission, she was cleared to enter the intensive care unit. What was more profound was she was able to stay with me additional days after surgery. My intensive care room at Emory included a suite area for my sister to stay in. The only stipulation was that she could not sleep in my room at night but could be with me during other times of the day. Not really certain of this fact, but I don't believe there was any other patient at Emory that had provisions made for them like God made for me. So, again, you can't tell me that my God won't make a way out of no way. Not only did I have my sister present during my surgery, but she was allowed to stay after surgery with her own sleeping quarters and additional days when I was removed from the Intensive Care Unit to a regular room.

Later on, after my discharge from Emory, my sister and I discussed all the amazing events that had occurred. Specifically, on the day before my surgery, I actually thought that she was burning the lines to Emory and making every effort to be by my side. But that was not the case because my brother, Alonzo, had convinced her it was a futile attempt since the established norms for every hospital nationwide was not to allow visitors due to the pandemic. As you can see, God was providentially moving on my behalf - breaking barriers, defying odds, opening and closing doors, and showing his sovereignty in mighty ways. Again, as we were thanking God, I could softly hear his words in my ear, "I will be with you."

Chapter 6

Process versus Promise

For all the promises of God in him are yea and in him Amen.
2 Corinthians 1:20

Is there anyone who will argue the undeniable truth that every product or species known to man must go through some type of process? Yet, when we apply this basic truth in the realm of spiritual development as believers, we would rather avoid or dismiss this important component. Who embraces the process of waiting? Who is not bothered by the pruning period that is necessary for growth? Who welcomes the suffering that will surely come our way or the pain encountered during our dry and difficult seasons of life? The real answer is that none of us want to be in this space. We would rather just move to the next step, which represents the promise: "the land that flows with milk and honey."

Be that as it may, as children of God, we must come to the understanding that the process is a necessary component that God lovingly takes us through for various reasons to lay hold on the promises ahead. According to ***James 1:2,*** we are to *"count it all joy when we fall into divers temptation."* Further, in verse 4, he says, *"Let patience have her perfect work, that ye may be* *perfect (mature) and complete wanting nothing."* Although this passage may be difficult to digest, in essence, it affirms that spiritual development takes place in the process of trials, especially when we find ourselves in difficult, unexpected, uncomfortable, or unfamiliar places.

Trusting the process is where our faith is tested. This has been a tangible lesson I had to learn throughout my personal journey of believing God for healing and wholeness. I have often heard that we have to trust God even when we can't trace him or know where he is leading us. I truly concur with this statement because that was what I had to do in order to lay hold on my promise of deliverance. I learned that faith does not necessarily make things easy; but faith does make impossible things possible.

Ironically, the process that leads to the expected promise often entails a purpose we can't see, don't understand, doesn't make sense, and drives us to unknown paths. Nonetheless, I have discovered that when we can fully understand our purpose in the midst of our trials, we are postured to humbly submit to God and yield to His divine will. A perfect example is Jesus, who knew His purpose here on earth and endured the pain, humiliation, suffering, and ultimately the crucifixion to fulfill the will of God. **Philippians 3:8** says, *"And being found in fashion as a man, he humbled himself, and became obedient unto death, even the death of the cross."* Jesus fully understood that his dying was for our eternal life. The purpose was what kept him on the cross when He had all the power necessary to come down and abort his mission. Thank you, Jesus, for the sacrifice and love you displayed just for me!!

Likewise, it is his divine purpose that fuels our faith and keeps us in the race to conform to His will. Going through the process is what challenges our faith, it pushes us to the brink when we have the Red Sea in front of us and Pharaoh's army behind us. It is the process stages that help to define our purpose in life. Subsequently, our purpose becomes our passion, and our passion gives life to our purpose. When we understand our divine purpose and assignment, then we are more willing to endure the process that eventually gets us to our expected end.

Jeremiah 29:11 states, *"For I know the thoughts that I have towards you, thoughts of peace and not evil to give you an expected end."* Interestingly enough, this is one of my favorite scriptures that I have memorized and constantly refer to when I need a booster shot.

Moreover, during my unforeseen period of illness, this scripture was rehearsed repeatedly in my mind, along with other healing scriptures, so I would not be consumed by the things I was facing. As a matter of fact, I have relied heavily on this scripture in Jeremiah to get me through some rough patches in my life. The thought of knowing my future is secure in God helps me not to get stuck in unfavorable situations, regardless of the things that come my way. As

David said in the book of ***Psalms 61***, when my heart is overwhelmed, lead me to that rock that is higher than I.

More often than not, it is through the pain, the waiting, the suffering, afflictions, disappointments, and other life challenges that we learn how to endure hardness as a good soldier. The process is the preparation room that enables us to possess the supernatural strength to move forward in search of God's many promises. More importantly, it is the process that brings light and life to the promise. It is in this place where we acknowledge the only certainty we have is God, His word, and His Spirit.

Interestingly enough, we have to trust the process because the process is full of "God Moments" displaying His sovereignty as we glimpse His magnificent power even in the most impossible and undesirable situations. I can truly say that throughout my ordeal of afflictions, I had the opportunity to see God's greatness displayed in countless dimensions. Henceforth, the conclusion of the matter is that God can work in the storms and processes of life to accomplish His ultimate purpose. We have a badge of honor in trusting God and the process that is attached to the promises He has made.

Chapter 7

Wilderness Experience

Be Still and know that I am God.
Psalms 46:10

Waiting on God to heal, deliver, and free us from life's uncomfortable situations is very challenging, to say the least. We would rather just quickly get to our desired end, as stated before. When I discovered that a tumor was on my brain, I was devastated. It was as if I had gone to sleep and experienced a nightmare. I just did not want to face this reality. But at the same time, I could no longer deny that my health was at risk. I was quickly thrust into a wilderness, which by definition means a dry place where there are limited resources for sustainability. Questions, fears, anxieties, and doubts flooded my mind while I struggled to hold onto my faith. I was in my wilderness with only one hope of survival, and that was to trust God. Believing that God already knew before I did that I would be at this juncture in my life, I had to trust Him to get me through this valley. The scripture I was given earlier at the start of 2020, "the just shall live by faith," was prophetic to my circumstance but would be that spiritual principle I would have to apply to lay hold of my miracle.

In the book of ***John 4:24***, there is the story of a woman who exhausted all of her resources from a bleeding condition she had for 12 years. She heard that Jesus was in her vicinity and determined within herself that she would be healed by touching the hem of Jesus' garment, and she did. This woman was in a dry place where life was no longer flourishing. She was experiencing a wilderness period of physical, social, and emotional affliction. She had many odds working against her, but with determination to overcome the barriers, she utilized her faith to believe that the impossible is possible, as she pushed herself to the place of healing and deliverance. As the story unfolds, Jesus felt the virtue of the woman's touch and affirmed that her faith had made her whole. This scripture was my lifeline to grab hold of that God is still able to deliver, heal, and set free. My thoughts were similar to this unidentified woman. If I could only touch the hem of Jesus' garment, I knew that I could be made whole too. My "hem of his garment" was the belief in God's word and the promise that He would be with me as he had said. My task was to keep the faith and wait on God's timing even in a place of discomfort.

The wilderness based on biblical teaching, refers to the children of Israel journeying to the promised land after being freed from Egyptian captivity. The wilderness became the temporary place of wandering in preparation for the promised land. Of course, their disobedience and self-pleasure caused their destiny to be delayed but there were many lessons learned in the wilderness as they experienced the many dimensions of Jehovah God. But another equally important doctrinal principle is that the "Wilderness

Experience" was never designed to be their permanent place of destination. When we find ourselves in an experience that can be parallel to wilderness wandering, just remember three important key concepts about what the wilderness can represent: 1) a solitary place for finding God's will and purpose, 2) a designed place and opportunity to personally witness God's mighty acts and unfailing love and 3) a designated time for a deepened level of understanding doctrinal truth about who God is and what He desires from us as his creation.

My wilderness experience became the journey of discovering and recovering from a rare tumor on my brain. As I reflect on my own story, the Monday of my surgery, I vaguely remember any specifics as I was rolled down for the operation. Having been prepped for surgery, I left my ICU room around 6:30 that morning, fading in and out of alertness. My sister and I had prayed earlier and were in agreement that God was covering me and the surgical team as they went about the task of removing the mass. Heaven was bombarded with prayers without ceasing by many of the saints of God.

I have to digress here and say thank you to all those who were interceding on my behalf. There were many people praying, including family members, my church family, coworkers, friends, and prayer warriors. The prayer warriors included people I knew and those I didn't know. But I am certain that prayers were bombarding God's throne on my behalf. The earnest and fervent prayers of the righteous availed much!

Around 9:30 on the day of surgery, Diane received a call in my ICU room that the surgery was about to begin and that the procedure would probably take about four to six hours, depending on what the doctors may have to do. No doubt my sister was confident in the prayers that had been made; but at the same time, she was probably full of anxiety since she was alone during that period of time waiting for the operation to be over and to hear the outcome. As the miraculous God we serve would have it, she received the second phone call, approximately two hours later at 11:30 a.m., informing her the surgery was over and that I was in the recovery room. The team of surgeons were able to go in and successfully remove all of the mass within the skull that was pressing on my brain in a much shorter span of time than they had originally thought it would take. They were very pleased with the outcome and would wait until I had fully recovered from the anesthesia to check my cognitive and memory skills, along with other medical side effects that could have been triggered by the surgery.

Shortly after recovery, I was able to identify who I was and where I was and responded correctly to all questions asked of me by my surgeon. The doctors, being pleased with my responses, affirmed to my sister in their words, "She is going to be all right." Once again, God had come through for me and answered many prayers offered on my behalf. Each daily evaluation by the doctors while in intensive care was an affirmation that I was progressing fine. Their daily visits were like clockwork. I would see one surgical doctor between 5:30 and 6:00 a.m. The other surgeon would visit me between 9:30 and 10:30 a.m. Each going through the routine of checking my cognitive skills, muscular strength, and progression from surgery.

Their visits were encouraging and reassuring that I was well on my way to a normal life. Three days later, I was moved out of intensive care into a regular room where I was regaining my strength and the ability to walk. During this period, I was evaluated for physical, occupational, speech, and cognitive therapy. My sister noted immediately after the surgery that my walking had significantly improved even with the use of a walking device, as I was walking normal without a stiffness on my left side, which was very evident before the surgery.

There were so many "only God moments" encountered during my experience as I walked this journey of faith into my expected outcome. As I mentioned earlier how, God had assured me with a whisper of his word that He would be with me. Well, he was just that and more in so many instances. In every action that occurred, I could see an awesome God at work. From the moment I received the news of the mass to the precaution and medication provided after the MRI, as well as instructions to go to the ER if I felt any strange or unusual sensation. And no, it doesn't stop there. The open door to get admitted into Emory for surgery by Dr. Johnson, to the ambulance attendants that transported me to the hospital who acted like big brothers, refusing to leave me alone in the lobby area of Emory until they visibly saw me rolled to intensive care with prayers that all would be well with me. Even Nurse Sara, who was charged with administering medical assistance in the intensive care unit and, in hindsight, played the role of my surrogate mother. God strategically had her in place consoling, praying, and encouraging me in the absence of my biological mother, who most definitely would have been there but resides in a nursing home, unable to do for herself.

There was never a moment that I felt alone. When my sister left my side on Thursday evening, I experienced something that was nothing short of a supernatural visit. While lying in bed, I was watching TV, and suddenly, I started seeing people entering my room. But the mystical occurrence is that they were not coming in through the physical door. It appeared as if they were coming in through the walls of my hospital room. At first, I thought I was hallucinating from the medicine, but that could not have been the case since there had been no changes in my medication, and this only occurred after my sister could not be with me. I was frantic because I could not explain this unusual situation. There were images of people coming into my small room as if they had been assigned to watch over me.

I could not naturally explain exactly what I was seeing. There was no communication or interaction with me from these images, just their presence. Because I was frightened, I tried not to focus on what was before my eyes, so I continued to engage myself by watching the TV. Occasionally, I would look to see if these images had left and saw they were still present. But two interesting figures stood out in my mind. A man who appeared to be sitting in a throne-like chair and a child who appeared at the foot of my bed. The child had his chin in his hand and was engaged in watching the TV along with me. It was only at this point that I felt my fears release. Long after this encounter, I gained spiritual insight that these images were a host of angels dispatched to fulfill the promise of God being with me so I would not be left alone.

Surely, God was on the scene in every way. Likewise, with day-to-day routine medical care, I can attest to the quality and expectations that Emory had of all employees for serving their patients. There was no lack of need. I would highly recommend this hospital based on my experience there. God had truly put me in the right hands for healing. During my hospital stay, a team of therapists was assigned to evaluate the need for physical, occupational, cognitive, and speech therapy. It was determined that I would need acute rehabilitation for a period of time before I could fully be back to my normal state. An answered prayer was for me to remain at Emory for the rehabilitation needed. Again, God provided the way for me to remain in Atlanta for admittance into Emory's Acute Rehabilitation Hospital. This was no small matter because there were several steps before I could get clearance into their facility, with the biggest issue being an available room and to my good fortune I was admitted. After entrance, I went through another series of assessments that Saturday. It was determined that I only needed physical and occupational therapy. "Glory Be to God!" He is Faithful to those who walk uprightly.

I was so advanced in meeting all of the objectives that the therapists had written for me to accomplish that the review team gave me clearance to be discharged on December 18th. I was praying to be home by Christmas if only the day before, but my amazing God made it possible for me to arrive home a week before Christmas. I became the "Christmas Miracle" of 2020.

Leaving Dublin afflicted and returning healed was nothing short of a miracle for those who were aware of my condition. So, everywhere I went and whatever I did when I arrived back in Dublin was about sharing the "Good News" of how God graciously led me out of the wilderness and valley of despair.

Returning to Dublin required additional rehabilitation for a period of time until all established goals were met. I was in the care of my sister and stayed with her until my visit in January with the surgeon to check on my progress. My baby sister took extremely great care of me and shared that I was a living testimony to the many prayers that were prayed. I want to pause and personally thank everyone who knew or did not know me but prayed for my healing and deliverance. I am here today based on God's will and your earnest prayers.

As God would have it, my sister and I spent Christmas 2020 together. This was a great bonding time for both of us. Christmas would be different this year anyway. We had lost Dad, and Diane had lost her husband, Kenny, in 2020. The familiar things done during Christmas with their presence in past years would be totally different in their absence. We never imagined that they would no longer be with us, but God knew and made it possible for us to be there for each other.

At Home for Christmas

Being home was nothing short of a miracle as I experienced a newness of life. I was overjoyed and sincerely grateful to have a normal life again welcoming a different state of mental, physical, and spiritual livelihood than my earlier crisis. Of course, for a period of time, home would be nestled in my sister's house as she continued her medical assistance with the best of care and an unselfish, loving spirit. Furthermore, anyone who knows my sister, Diane, can identify that she is an immaculate housekeeper, decorator and caregiver. Needless to say, I felt like a queen entreated with the luxury of her care. Oh yeah, there were times she was a bit bossy, but I knew she had my best interest in mind. Honestly, for me, it was a humbling experience since I was so accustomed to taking care of my own needs and living in my own environment. This too, became a teachable moment because at some point in life we may have to depend on someone else to accommodate what may be lacking in our life. God strategically had my sister in place to fill all gaps in helping me through the recovery and rehabilitation process. Getting me to scheduled appointments and therapy were no small tasks and is a reminder how far love goes to be of service. Yes it is simply amazing how God orchestrates every facet of life, giving special attention to every need and provisions required.

To shift gears a bit, Christmas has always been a joyous occasion for the Edwards family. For the most part, all of our families looked forward to being home for Christmas. This tradition was established by our parents as they planned with much loving details and preparation for the arrival of their children, wives, husbands, and grandchildren. They spared no expense in making sure each Christmas season was special and memorable. Mom's dressing, giblet gravy, baked turkey, a variety of cakes and pies, ambrosia, and all the other trimmings were a scrumptious delight. Dad always made sure we had fruits, pecans, syrup, oxtails, and any other specialty that was unique to each adult child. It was always our parent's greatest pleasure and a gift from God to have all of their eight children together again in their home. The smiles on their faces were priceless as they had another opportunity to share joyous moments with their children, grandchildren, and extended families.

Over the years as our parents began to age, the children kept the tradition alive by doing the things we knew made Christmas meaningful to them and to us. As each sibling family expanded, some changes were inevitable and smaller Christmas gatherings at home replaced the larger settings we were so familiar with. Nonetheless, the highlight of Christmas was seeing mom and dad open their gifts from their adult children and spouses, and of course, the grandchildren. That tradition didn't change, even though the setting was somewhat different. As mentioned earlier, Christmas 2020 was very different without our patriarch, Daddy, but our Christmas seasons will always be memorable in the legacy and love he had for his family. My mother, who is still alive by the grace of God, planted an invaluable seed of love and commitment to family that also flourishes in the Edwards spiritual legacy to this day and will remain throughout every season of life. Because Christmas represents the life-giver, it will always be a joyous time of year because of the countless privileges, blessings, abundance, mercy, and favor God bestowed on the Edwards family! Undeniably, that is why being home for Christmas was my special prayer and returning home in a much better state of health, indeed was my miracle as a gift from above. To God be the Glory!!!!

Post Surgery

My next scheduled appointment after surgery and acute rehabilitation at Emory was on January 5th, where my surgeon, Dr. Jeffrey Olsen, revealed the findings of the pathology report. I was diagnosed with a rare tumor called Hemangiopericytoma. I am certain the doctor explained to me what type of tumor this was, but it was too much for me to process at the time. As a result, I had to do my own medical research just to determine what I was dealing with. Hemangiopericytoma of the brain is a rare soft tissue that forms from the inner lining of the brain. There are only two types of this tumor: stages II or III. The report showed that the tumor was stage II. The medical plan was to have six weeks of radiation treatment to destroy all tumor cells that may cause the tumor beds to grow again. The surgeons were able to remove all of the tumor that was in my skull area but did not want to get too close to its roots in the lining of the brain.

The next phase of the healing journey was to go through radiation. My surgeon introduced me to Dr. Bree Eaton, an oncologist at Emory, who would be taking over my medical needs. Dr. Eaton further explained the type of tumor I had and recommended that I receive proton therapy, which is designed to target specific areas of radiation to the affected area. I began my first treatment on February 16, 2021, and was very fortunate to stay with my brother, Don, and his wife, Tina, to avoid traveling the distance from Dublin to Atlanta, which is about 150 miles one way. They graciously opened their home for me to live with them and provided daily transportation during the six weeks of radiation. It was also during this period that we had opportunities to rebuild our relationship as adult siblings and recall memories of our childhood experiences. This open door was indeed a reminder that God was with me, and it was encouraging to know that I could count on my family to be there when I needed them the most. This principle of love for family was instilled in us by our parents at an early age.

The actual experience encountered with the radiation therapy was not bad at all. I really didn't know what to expect. I thought it would be painful, but it was not at all. The most challenging part of the procedure was the mask that was fitted to my face, strapped on so tightly to prevent any movement of my head. The precision of the radiation was key and the mask was necessary to treat me properly and not damage other areas that did not require radiation. In actuality, the time of travel to the center was significantly much longer than the actual radiation therapy itself which was about ten minutes or less. The large cylinder tunnel that I was in and the tiny gurney pale in comparison to other experiences I had encountered. However, any fears during this process were overcome by listening to worship melodies through the headphones provided. No doubt, the music of praise and scriptures memorized helped me through this "dreaded den" that enclosed my body.

Chapter 8

Brokenness

The Lord is nigh unto them that are of a broken heart and saveth such as be of a contrite spirit.
Psalms 34:18

Brokenness is another component that God uses to draw us closer to him so that we are fitted for His use. ***Ephesians 2:10*** states, *"for we are his workmanship, created in Christ Jesus unto good works which God hath before ordained that we should walk in them."* Sometimes, it is the will of God that we go through seasons where life leaves us in a broken state only to come face to face with an Almighty God that has purposed us to something greater as citizens of His Kingdom. In the book of Jeremiah, we find this biblical principle on display. We are all merely clay in the potter's hand that is marred by sin, fleshly influences, and worldly distractions. As ***Jeremiah 18:2*** states, *"Arise and go down to the potter's house, and there I will cause thee to hear my words."* Verse 4 states, *"And the vessel that he made was marred in the hand of the potter: so he made it again another vessel, as seemed good to the potter to make it."* From this passage of scripture, Jeremiah was to learn a valuable and enduring lesson as he observed the potter with the pottery on the wheel. The significance of this message is to reveal that it is often in a place of brokenness where we sense the urgency of yielding to the potter to be reshaped and fashioned as he desires. Often, there are flaws in our life that require repentance, forgiveness, and a spiritual rebirth before we can move and respond to the call of God over our life.

The Bible has many references to Old and New Testament witnesses who experienced brokenness in their journey of accepting and fulfilling the call and plan of God. Time will not allow me to go over the litany of people God used to reveal His Glory and to show how insufficient and helpless we are without Him in our life. Brokenness was certainly a lesson learned as I traveled this uncharted path that God led me on. When you have experienced the mountaintop blessings and favor of God and all of a sudden life shifts and now you find yourself walking through the valley of the shadow of death, the question is "What are you going to do?" Do you run from God, or do you run to Him which is the only right thing to do.

If my spiritual foundation had not been firmly established in God, His word, and faith in His word, I would not have been able to make it through my valley season. Marvin Sapp put to music a song entitled "I Never Would Have Made It." No doubt this song was born out of his own difficult and uncomfortable places. You see, each of us has our own story of struggles and hardships. How we perceive our circumstances during these trying times and messy situations helps us to respond in the right manner. When we step into the light of God and allow Him to expose our brokenness, we are well on our way to the road of healing and wholeness. Drawing nigh to God draws Him nearer to us. Indeed, God specializes in putting broken pieces back together again!

I can truly relate to the lyrics penned by the gospel artist Marvin Sapp because brokenness causes one to be in pain, suffering from some challenge that seems insurmountable, or puts you in a state of mind that causes emotional unrest. For me, brokenness was a defining moment. I had to literally come to grips with the understanding that my life had taken on an unusual yet supernatural turn. God had to help me re-evaluate priorities and to recognize my own insufficiencies.

The experiences taught me many lessons as I stayed in His word and presence. I saw layers of carnality that needed to be peeled off. I had to revisit different periods of my personal spiritual journey with repentance, confession, and a genuine search for divine identity. I was seeking God earnestly to be who he had created me to be. Yet, in the midst of all that had been encountered at this twist in my life, the most valuable lesson I learned was that brokenness can be the seed of blessings which eventually leads to divine destiny.

Chapter 9

Enduring Faith

Having a successful surgery and achieving all of the therapy goals to regain my independence at home, I was next faced with the radiation treatment stage, simply because this rare tumor could be aggressive. This knowledge did not cause the initial anxiety I had from my first discovery of a mass. Because God had displayed his faithfulness, He enabled me to endure this treatment with the prayers and support of loved ones and friends. Each day from the start of treatment, I continued to begin my day with praise, worship, and communion with God. I continued reading devotionals that kept my focus on God and not my circumstances. Ironically, my cousin, Evelyn Carswell, who also resides in Atlanta, was the vessel God used to propel my faith during my acute rehabilitation and radiation treatment period. Diane, having fulfilled her assignment, was back in Dublin and would call periodically, as well as my older sister, Sharon, and her daughter, Lakeshia. My brothers Alonzo, Ira Jr. & Glen called periodically to check on my well-being. My brother and sister-in-law, Don and Tina, provided lodging and companionship in Atlanta. Their children, Courtney and Taneisha, along with the grandchildren, made visits to check on their Aunt Pat during my stay in Atlanta. Steve, Alonzo, and my nephew, Colin, ensured I always had a way to get to my scheduled appointments from Dublin to Atlanta when there was a need. I intentionally share these details to make a point that I had a great support system with my family. In many cases, separated by distance, their personal life, and the pandemic period, God made sure I was never left alone or in need of anything. Knowing I had their love, prayers, and support was my daily dose of medicine.

Interestingly enough, it was my cousin, Evelyn Carswell, who kept me spiritually grounded. We didn't talk or see each other every day, nor was there a need to do so. However, the quality of time and efforts made to communicate with each other were priceless. She became my confidant and sounding board whenever I felt the need to express my inner thoughts or just share a sentiment of the graciousness of a caring, loving God.

Early on during my stay in Emory's Acute Rehab Hospital, still under the COVID-19 restriction, I had many phone calls from family members, friends, and co-workers who were a great source of encouragement for me to trust God the more. However, my cousin Evelyn was the primary vessel God used to pray with me, cry with me, and listen to me as I shared my deepest fears and overcoming victories. It was actually Evelyn who uncannily dropped the seed of writing a book based on the many testimonies that I shared with her on frequent phone conversations about how God had already done some miraculous events in my life since the beginning of my health issues in Atlanta. Initially, I was very reluctant to the very thought of writing a book and had convinced myself that this was not a part of my skill set or interest. In fact, I was even annoyed at this suggestion and remember dismissing it from my mind the very moment it was spoken. But God began to deal with me, and every time I would share my testimony, others would also confirm that I should write a book. After delayed obedience to God, I eventually surrendered to this assignment. As I embarked on another journey that was so foreign to me, I saw God's loving hand in the midst while I was yet going through my restoration season.

As God would have it, cousin Evelyn dropped off a care box filled with all kinds of items, including delightful snacks, during my rehab period. But two devotional books entitled "The Lord is My Shepherd" and "Unafraid" were a divine source of nourishment, encouragement, and deliverance that kept my mind on God's word, even in a broken place of affliction. I read the first devotional, "The Lord is my Shepherd" each day during my acute rehab at Emory. As I read this devotional daily, I would write in my journal the inspirational messages shared and my personal affirmations for that day. With pandora music in the air, the daily word, and my personal prayers, I was armed to face whatever the challenge might be because my Shepherd was with me! Ironically, the first devotional got me through all of the therapy days in Atlanta and the therapy I had to do in Dublin. When it was time for my radiation treatment, the second devotional book, "Unafraid" was divinely ordered to be my daily dose of faith-filled words to combat any fears during this period. During the reading of this book, every scripture and inspirational message was so relevant and kept me with God's amazing peace. God's providential hand had gone before me through my cousin's selection of these devotionals to give me the peace, reassuring faith, and victory required to overcome the radiation stage of my healing. Truly God was restoring my soul from a place of brokenness and affliction. The faith to endure my challenges in the various forms they appeared became a part of the road to complete healing. I had come to far by the grace of God to give up or give in. After six weeks of radiation treatment, God had allowed me to successfully complete this phase of my faith journey.

Chapter 10

The Power of God's Word

It is written; man shall not live by bread alone but by every word that proceeds out of the mouth of God.
Luke 4:4

There was no doubt that the word of God kept me grounded, hopeful, and steadfast in the faith during the most turbulent period of my life. Of course, there were days after my diagnosis that I felt empty and void of any faith, not having a sense of why my world had turned upside down. Honestly, it was not knowing the outcome of a dreaded sickness that grabs hold and beats you down to a pulp, as my mind would have me to believe. When your faith tells you one thing but reality counteracts all the faith you thought you possessed. Nevertheless, it was at this juncture that I had to grab hold of something that was much bigger and more powerful than my current fears. That something for me was the promises of God's unchanging word. **Hebrew 4:12** states, "*the word of God is quick and powerful, sharper than any two-edged sword; piercing even to the dividing of soul and spirit, of both joints and marrow, and is able to discern the thoughts and intentions of the heart.*" In simple terms, God's word always reflects the awesomeness of his power and is always relevant, no matter what the circumstance may be.

Subsequently, everyone has to come under the authority of the spoken, written and spirit-filled word of God. The truth of the matter is that our almighty and powerful God sees and knows everything regardless of its visibility or lack thereof. Nothing or no one can stand against God or His word that represents his divinity, his sovereignty, and Lordship over all creation and, more importantly, mankind. *"For the earth is the Lord's and the fullness thereof, the world and they that dwell therein(**Psalms 24:1.**)"*

David captured the essence of this truth in the multiple scriptures written in the book of Psalms. *"When my heart is overwhelmed, lead me to the Rock that is higher than I (**Psalms 61:2**)."; "Be Still and know that I am God (**Psalms 46:10**)"; "The Lord is my light and my salvation whom shall I fear. The Lord is the strength of my life of whom shall I be afraid*(**Psalms 27:1-2**)*"*. *"The Lord is my Shepherd and I shall not want (**Psalms 23**)"; "Forever O Lord, thou word is settled in Heaven (**Psalms 119:89**)."* Moreover, **Proverbs 18:10** states, *"The name of the Lord is a strong tower, the righteous run to it and is safe."* Jesus himself states in **Mark 9:23** that *"All things are possible to them that believe."*

Scriptures such as these and countless others, whether memorized or read anew, kept my drifting faith alive and became the lifeline that anchored my soul with certainty that the God I trusted would not fail me. The various stages of healing beginning with my diagnosis, then surgery, rehabilitation, radiation, and last of all seizure attacks, were challenges that were too big for me but not for God. Clinging to His word and verbally declaring it in my mind, and speaking the word out loud was the source of my miracle. The word of God indeed became my daily nourishment and helped to calm my fears, anxieties, and discomforts and brought a sense of undeniable peace as I walked through my valley of the shadows of death. Truly it was God who kept me and would not let me go. It is my personal testimony that nothing can compare to being sustained by the word of God. I am thankful that knowing and studying the word of God was a type of precursor and preparation for the affliction that suddenly came upon me to attack my mind, body, soul, and spirit. Much of God's word I had begun learning as a child but was later cultivated through church teachings, self-study, and spiritual growth. So, the seed of his rich word was planted and watered as God gave the increase with experience, spiritual wisdom, and enlightenment. Indeed, it was prayers and faith coupled with God's word that brought me out of the horrible pit that I was in. Glory be to God that I am standing here today only because my Loving, Caring, Powerful God made a way!!!!!

My spiritual counsel to anyone when I have an opportunity to share my testimony is that you never want to live your life apart from God. The sooner you grasp this truth, the better your life will be. God wants the very best for mankind, and He delights in giving us all the things needed to live a healthy and prosperous life here on earth. It is His pleasure to care for us and meet our every need. The scriptures tell us in *1 Corinthian 2:9-10* *"that eyes have not seen;*

nor ears have heard the things that God has prepared for those that love Him. But he has revealed the mystery of his will to the children of His Kingdom." Therefore, it is crucial for everyone to read and study his word so we can know his will and the rich heritage that has been freely given to mankind. Truly, there is much power in the word of God.

Chapter 11

Grateful

In everything, give thanks: for this is the will of God in Christ Jesus concerning you.
1 Thessalonians 5:18

You can ask me on any given day now, "How are you doing?" My response in most cases would be, "I AM GRATEFUL." WHY?

I have so much to be thankful for. Looking back from September 3rd of 2020 until this present moment, my life was altered forever, and yet even in the midst of what I encountered, I am still here by the grace of God. What appeared to be the end of my chapter in life with an unexpected, rare tumor residing in my brain became a faith journey of rediscovering God in the many dimensions of His glory and nature as I also had many quiet moments to reassess my relationship with him and identity as a believer.

Experiences are only valuable if you take the time to learn lessons and teachable moments. In my case, there were numerous lessons learned. Never take life for granted. Never feel you can't be touched by the evils, struggles, and pains of life. Never be caught up in self-reliance because you don't know who you will need to help you along the way. Never be overconfident, no matter how blessed and favored you may feel, because seasons do change. Learn to appreciate the little things in life. Additionally, learn to be compassionate and sensitive to the needs of others. Give time and attention to hearing from God daily as he wants and desires to commune with you. Always remember to be thankful in whatever situation you are in because someone else may be less fortunate than you. Well, I could go on and on and on with tidbits of nuggets to chew on as result of my own personal experiences gleaned. The litany of lessons learned are enormous and invaluable. And yet, I am stronger, wiser, and better because I went through this valley. I was tried in the fire, but I came out as pure gold. I am not boasting about myself but grateful to God that I did not have to go through my afflictions without leaning and depending on Him daily to bring me out. God has always been there for me in the most critical times of life, but this health battle has been by far the biggest hurdle to leap over. And yet, I found out in a more personal way that there is no problem or situation that is bigger than God. Our God IS BIG, BIG, BIG!!!!

So, use your struggles in life as a tool to help others and refuse to nurse things that may not be going well with you. See things for what they are but, more importantly, see things through the lens of what could be. There are so many possibilities that await us, but if we only limit ourselves to what we already know we become trapped, not allowing God to stretch us. During my health ordeal, admittedly, I was stretched beyond my finite being. It was only God that could get me from point A to point B. Knowing that prayers, love, and support were undergirding me, I, like the disciple Peter, had to step out of the boat in the midst of a raging and boisterous sea. I, like Peter, got distracted by the surrounding environment that appeared to be a threat to life and had to cry out, "Lord, Save Me." Yet in the greatest despair, God was there to rescue Peter, and God was there to rescue me. Peter's encounter of walking on the water was recorded for our learning. His fears, distractions, and lack of faith are recorded to show our insufficiency at best. I learned that God knows all about us and is always on the scene to hear our faintest cries, no matter the circumstances.

I have often said that the same God that can deliver us from a pending crisis is the same God that can deliver us in the midst of a circumstance. God delivered the children of Israel in the middle of their wilderness wandering; He delivered the three Hebrew boys, Shadrack, Meshack, and Abednego, while in the midst of a fiery furnace heated seven times hotter than usual. Likewise, Daniel was delivered in the middle of a den with hungry lions.

Each situation and many similar recorded passages of scriptures attest to the intentions of the enemy to defeat, destroy, and annihilate God's divine will over the lives of those who took a firm stand in their faith and had a secure relationship with God. Now I know without a doubt the truth of this statement that God is able to do exceedingly, abundantly, above all that we think or even ask of Him, according to the power that works within us. ***(Ephesians 3:20).*** The myriad of experiences I encountered added value to my faith and trust in an unfailing God. Thus, my response to God, in all that occurs in life, is to have a grateful spirit. I shall never forget what God has done for me. I will earnestly make my boast in the Lord and declare his goodness among men.

In conclusion, my personal testimony is that God gave me a "Christmas Miracle" in the valley of the shadow of death. I can truly say "Yes Lord, to your will and to your way". You are the Rock of my Salvation, and I am so grateful because you brought me through, even when I was in a horrible pit. I am so thankful for the following revelation and spiritual insight that resonate in my spirit man today.

- "Messy situations" are never too big for God! There is always a message in the messiness of life.
- God majors in giving purpose and order to our lives even when we encounter calamities, setbacks, disappointments, distractions, and detours.
- "Life is never a straight line." That's why faith is such an integral part and essential component of our walk with Christ.
- God is still writing our stories. Mishaps will come our way, but it is never over until God closes the Book of Life.

- God can take our "valley experiences" and give us "victory over our circumstances.
- We are his special workmanship and are always eternally secure when we remain in the "potter's hand."

There will be times in life when faith-believers will be tasked to rediscover the joy of the Lord beyond the calamities of life, knowing that it is always in our weakness that He is made strong. However, when our will is aligned with His will, we can trust God even during the most difficult processes of our spiritual development. For in His presence is fullness of joy! Therefore, we can count our many blessings and will find that there is so much more of a reason to be thankful than not. If we just look for the everyday miracles of life right in front of us, we can attest to the truth that God is good and surely, his goodness and mercy will follow us all the days of our life. As I look back over my life and begin to think things over, I can truly say that I am blessed; I have a testimony!!!!!!

My Healing Scriptures

The LORD is my shepherd; I shall not want.
Psalm 23:1

The LORD is my light and my salvation; whom shall I fear? The LORD is the strength of my life; of whom shall I be afraid?
Psalms 27:1

He that dwelleth in the secret place of the most High shall abide under the shadow of the Almighty. I will say of the LORD, He is my refuge and my fortress: my God; in him will I trust.
Psalm91:1-2

Be still and know that I am God: I will be exalted among the heathen, I will be exalted in the earth. The LORD of hosts is with us; the God of Jacob is our refuge. Selah.
Psalm 46:10-11

Many of the afflictions of the righteous: but the LORD delivereth him out of them all.
Psalm 34:19

The name of the LORD is a strong tower: the righteous runneth into it and is safe.
Prover 18:10

So, then faith cometh by hearing, and hearing by the word of God
Romans 10:17

And this is the confidence that we have in him, that, if we ask any thing according to his will, he heareth us: And if we know that he hear us, whatsoever we ask, we know that we have the petitions that we desired of him.
1 John 5:14-15

The entrance of your words giveth light; it giveth understanding unto the simple.
Psalm 119:130

So shall my word be that goeth forth out of my mouth: it shall not return unto me void, but it shall accomplish that which I please, and it shall prosper in the thing whereto I sent it.
Isaiah 55:11

For I know the thoughts that I think toward you, saith the LORD, thoughts of peace, and not evil to give you an expected end.
Jeremiah 29:11

No weapon that is formed against thee shall prosper; and every tongue that shall rise against thee in judgement thou shall condemn. This is the heritage of the servants of the LORD, and their righteousness is of me, saith the LORD.
Isaiah 54:17

But he was wounded for our transgressions, he was bruised for our iniquities: the chastisement of our peace was upon him; and with his stripes we are healed.
Isaiah 53:5

Who his own self bare our sins in his body on the tree, that we, being dead to sins, should live unto righteousness: by whose strips ye were healed.

1 Peter 2:24

Confess your faults one to another, and pray one for another, that you may be healed. The effectual fervent prayer of a righteous man availeth much.
James 5:16

He that is our God is the God of salvation; and unto GOD the Lord belong the issues from death.
Psalm 68:20

A Prayer Of Faith

Most Holy and gracious Father, we come before your throne room with a heart of gratitude and lips of thanksgiving! God, we sincerely thank you for all of your manifold blessings and we offer unto to you praise, glory, and honor.

We magnify your name because your word lets us know that you are the almighty God. You are everlasting to everlasting! There is no God like you. No one, nowhere, nothing above, or beneath the earth can stand against your Lordship, Kingdom, and Power! Your sovereignty rules and your providential hand goes before us.

So, God, we say thank you for being Abba Father, our daddy, that cares for us. We are the sheep of your pasture. We can go in and out feeding on your green pasture. You enable us to lie down beside the still, tranquil waters. We are privileged to drink from the fountain of life as you lead us in the pathway of righteousness. Even during the times when we find ourselves in the valley of turmoil and despair, we won't fear because you promised us that you are forever with us.

You are the restorer of our soul. You daily load us with benefits and precious promises:

- We are the head and not the tail
- We are the lenders and not the borrowers
- We are above and not beneath our circumstances

- We are more than conquerors because of our love for you
- We know when the enemy comes in like a flood, you will lift up a standard against him
- We know nothing is impossible to them that believe; for we walk by faith and not by sight
- We can look to the hills from which cometh our help for our help comes from you, Lord.
- You are the light of our salvation; you are the strength of our life and we will not be afraid
- You know what we need even before we ask and you delight in giving good gifts to your children
- You are able to do exceedingly, abundantly, above all that we ask or even think, according to the power within us.
- Greater is He that is in us than he that is in the world

So now we ask God to release your glory! Your glory represents the weight of your presence. It represents all that you are, all that you have been and all that you will be!

Most Holy God, we rest our cares at your feet because you care for us in every area of our life. Help us to trust you even more. Even so, come Lord Jesus!

REFLECTION AND EXPLORATION QUESTIONS

1. *There are various components that shape our character, values, and core existence, which help propel us through life. What are some critical and necessary tools that have grounded and established your seed of faith to persevere?*

_____
_____
_____
_____
_____
_____
_____
_____
_____
_____
_____
_____
_____
_____
_____
_____
_____
_____

2. *How do you focus on the promise when the process becomes overwhelming and, at times delayed? How do you find the inner strength to move beyond the weeds without getting stuck in a temporary place?*

3. *Faith believers have to find God in a solitary way and our encounter is personalized as our knowledge of God grows at a deeper level. Oftentimes, the deeper dimensions of God are experienced in some of the most difficult and trying times. What experiences in your faith journey have resulted in a deeper and rewarding manner of seeing the supernatural manifestation of an Almighty God?*

4. *Miracles are God's visible and tangible supernatural gifts afforded to mankind. However, the backdrop to miracles stems from impossible situations and hopeless circumstances. Can you recall a time when only God could have made an impossible situation possible?*

Additions To My Life

But seek ye first the kingdom of God, and his righteousness; and all these things shall be added unto you. Matthew 6:33

There have been so many impactful additions to my life based on the promises of God. I would be remiss if I did not make mention of some very special people God added to my life during my "affliction season". In their own loving way, God had them in place to serve specific needs in my life. Much thanks for your love and support rendered.

Esther Walker
Laverne Jones
Debra Wright
Gail Wilbur
Debra Walker
Carol Salem
Reverend Elgin & Terri Dixon
Minister Anthony & Natalie Fields
Evelyn Rozier
Marie Jackson
Superintendent Larry & Supervisor Larance Gordon
Advantage Rehab Therapists
Rudolph Thomas
Andy Wright
Jasmine Watson & Jalen Bartee
Alexis George
Merlene Swint

Donna Harmon
Minister Delois Moss
Judy Smith
Gladys Edwards
Fairview Outpatient Therapists
Missionary Jacqueline Millander
Missionary Mary Walden
Evangelist Mary Foreman
Superintendent James & District Missionary Bell
Pastor Dorothy Simmons & Stanley Family
Dublin City Schools Central Office Staff
Jordan Grove Church Family
Tau Omicron Omega Chapter, Alpha Kappa Alpha, Inc.

BOOK REFERENCES

- *Blueletterbible.com*

- *Biblestudytools.com*

- *Dictionary.com*

- *Olivetree.com*

- *Strongs Exhaustive Bible Concordance Online Bible Study Tools*

- *"Unafraid" Grace Malone*